Go Outside!

GO FOR A
HIKE!

By Peter Finn

Gareth Stevens
PUBLISHING

Please visit our website, www.garethstevens.com. For a free color catalog of all our high-quality books, call toll free 1-800-542-2595 or fax 1-877-542-2596.

Library of Congress Cataloging-in-Publication Data

Names: Finn, Peter, 1978- author.
Title: Go for a hike! / Peter Finn.
Description: New York : Gareth Stevens Publishing, [2020] | Series: Go outside! | Includes index.
Identifiers: LCCN 2019009906| ISBN 9781538244852 (pbk.) | ISBN 9781538244876 (library bound) | ISBN 9781538244869 (6 pack)
Subjects: LCSH: Hiking–Juvenile literature.
Classification: LCC GV199.52 .F56 2020 | DDC 796.51–dc23
LC record available at https://lccn.loc.gov/2019009906

Published in 2020 by
Gareth Stevens Publishing
111 East 14th Street, Suite 349
New York, NY 10003

Editor: Therese Shea
Designer: Sarah Liddell

Photo credits: Cover, pp. 1, 5, 7, 23 Monkey Business Images/Shutterstock.com; p. 9 Rawpixel.com/Shutterstock.com; p. 11 kos.rar/Shutterstock.com; pp. 13, 24 (poison ivy) Kyle Selcer/Shutterstock.com; p. 15 Bruce MacQueen/Shutterstock.com; pp. 17, 24 (waterfall) Sinelev/Shutterstock.com; pp. 19, 24 (picnic) JCStudio/Shutterstock.com; p. 21 Zachary Hoover/Shutterstock.com.

Printed in the United States of America

Some of the images in this book illustrate individuals who are models. The depictions do not imply actual situations or events.

CPSIA compliance information: Batch #CW20GS: For further information contact Gareth Stevens, New York, New York at 1-800-542-2595.

Contents

My name is Emma.
I hike with my family.

We hike in the woods.

I carry a map.
It tells us where to go.

We follow a path called a trail. We don't want to get lost!

We see many plants.
There's poison ivy.
Don't touch it!

13

We see many animals.
There's a deer.
Don't scare it!

We hike by a waterfall!
We take a picture.

We stop for lunch.
Dad packed a picnic!

We clean up our trash.
We leave no trace!

Hiking is fun!
Go for a hike!

Words to Know

picnic   poison ivy   waterfall

Index

24